T0370313

PICTURE YOUR
Dreams
Goals & Plans

DENISE FARQUHARSON

This book is dedicated to my dreamers.
My husband Louis and my beautiful children
Louis Junior, Antoinette & Alexander

Order this book online at www.trafford.com
or email orders@trafford.com

Most Trafford titles are also available at major online book retailers.

Print information available on the last page.

ISBN: 978-1-4251-2223-2 (sc)

Trafford rev. 12/10/2018

 www.trafford.com

North America & international
toll-free: 1 888 232 4444 (USA & Canada)
fax: 812 355 4082

Acknowledgments

Frances Farquharson, Mark and Lynda, Tony Pedley, Rosanna & Leslie
Daniel Gillespie, Sandra Smith, Clare Simpson, Jag Rai & family.

Thanks for your commitment to my dream,
your encouraging words and belief in me.

*"Write the vision and make it plain upon tablets,
so that he may run that readeth it."*

The book of Habakkuk Chapter 2, Verse 2
King James Version of the Bible

Contents

Dreams, Goals & Plans

Everyone has a dream about someone or something. What is your dream?

The definition of a dream is an ambition; cherished desire; or an ideal that drives you.

Dreams are for any one regardless of race, gender or colour. Your dreams could be wildly different from someone else's but they are unique and belong to you.

So how are you going to make them come true?

Well that is where this book comes in; of how to 'Picture Your Dreams, Goals and Plans'. Here you can start to collect a futuristic scrapbook of all the things that you desire.

How to get started

Spend time alone with just a pen and paper and write down the dreams you have already floating around in your head.

Think about why you want to have it. Consider what you will feel like to achieve it.

Write down some possible challenges you may face to achieve that dream and some actions you will have to put in place to solve those challenges.

Set some dreams that can be achieved in a week, month or a year.
If you can achieve the small dreams, then the medium and long term dreams will seem easier to look forward to.

Pictures, Photos and Visualise!

Get lots of them. Start to build a collection of the things you want to achieve. Cut them out of magazines, brochures, photo album or clipart.

Pictures will paint the dream for you and gives you something to visualise whilst you are trying your best to achieve it.

Pictures will help you refocus when something goes wrong or when it looks like you will not achieve that dream. Pictures will help to make the dream come true.

Examples of some dreams and the pictures you can use

It is estimated that an average person has 10,000 thoughts or images going through their mind each day. A number of these pictures are you desiring something or seeing where you could be in maybe 5 years time, or even as soon as 3 months time.

Take a look at some of the pictures on the front cover. Are these some of the dreams you have for your future?

Let's see how can you turn those dreams into pictures of your destiny and be a step closer to it all coming true.

6

Dream:
To make more money at work or in business.

Picture:
Place a photograph of the amount of money or yourself holding it.

Dream:
Publishing or writing a book.

Picture:
Have a picture of the possible book cover or a sample chapter.

Dream:
To be on holiday in the Caribbean.

Picture:
Get pictures of the Caribbean from travel brochures.

Dream:
See the wonders of the world.

Picture:
Get the picture of the amazing country you need to visit.

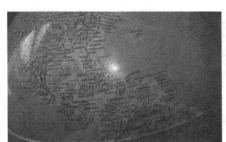

Dream:
Travel to various places in the world.

Picture:
A picture of the country and a picture of you beside it.

Dream:
To go to Disney in Florida, USA.

Picture:
Get pictures of Mickey Mouse or brochures of Florida from the travel agent.

Dream:
Playing a musical instrument

Picture:
A picture of you playing or a picture of the instrument.

Dream:
To have a brand new home.

Picture:
An example of the type of home with the building style you would like to have.

Dream:
Drive a top of the range car.

Picture:
Get some pictures of the car you want from car showrooms or magazines.

Dream:
Wear nice designer clothes.

Picture:
Get some pictures of your favourite pieces. Place your photograph on them.

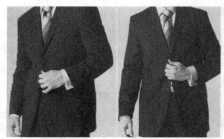

Once my pictures are in place what do I do next?

Share your dream with others.
Find others that you can trust who will support you on your dream journey. Talk with them on a regular basis so that they can help to monitor your progress.

Some will give you advice which may sound like discouragement but they might be pre-warning you of potential pitfalls. Make sure you listen to them carefully. Unfortunately, there will be some who will try to discourage you. But you have to ignore them and move on.

Keep looking at the picture
Keep your book close by so that you can look at your dreams regularly. Make sure the goals and plans are being achieved. If they are not, then reset them.

You might even find that the original dream does not fit your current lifestyle or beliefs. So you might have to change it completely or create a similar dream with new plans and goals that will stretch you again, but will still be achievable.

What if I don't achieve my dream?

Do not be disappointed if your dream is not achieved. That can happen to anyone, for all sorts of reasons: money, health, family changes.

If it is possible then reset your goals with a new date. Take another look at the goals and plans and make sure they are reasonable.

But don't just leave it at that, go back to the section called 'How to Get Started'. Begin to visualise again. Read some of the positive quotes at the top of your dream pages and get some new and fresh ideas.

How to fill in your dream book

Each page has the following:-

• Date Set
This is the date that you put the dream picture into your book.

• Date Achieved
When your dream is achieved, write down the date.
It is no longer a picture or photo in your book but has now become a reality.

• Goals, Plans
Write down simple, achievable steps to make your dream real.

Example:

The **dream** is to go on a safari.

The weekly **plan** is to set aside a certain amount of money each month.

The **goal** is to achieve a certain amount of money within a year. At the end of the year you will have enough money to book the safari dream holiday of a lifetime.

• Notes
This is for you to add anything you like. You may want to write down the reasons why you want the dream to come true, or a person who inspired the dream in you.

EXAMPLE

Description of My Dream

Go to Kenya, Africa in 2009 and have a 5 day safari and see the animals, especially the tigers in their natural habitat.

Date Set

1st Dec 2006

Date Achieved

2nd February, 2009

Goals & Plans

What I will do to achieve my dream.

Plan – Starting Dec 2006, I will save £100 a month and put it in a savings account.

Goal – I will save £2,400 by Dec 2008 and book the Safari Dream Holiday.

Notes

My grandfather always told me about the African safari. He painted a beautiful picture in my mind that made me want to experience it myself. Now my dream has become a reality –Yes!

MY DREAM PAGES

SOME HAVE THEIR DREAMS TAKEN AWAY JUST BY ONE NEGATIVE STATEMENT,
DON'T LET ANYONE TAKE YOURS AWAY.

STAY FOCUSED, STAY ON THE PATH, STAY WITH YOUR DREAM

THE ONLY PERSON WHO CAN STOP YOU IS YOU

WHEN THINGS DON'T GO THE WAY YOU EXPECT.
EXPECT TO DO SOMETHING DIFFERENT THE NEXT TIME.

SOME SAY DREAMING IS SILLY, BUT A SILLY DREAM CREATED A LIGHT BULB!

DO TODAY WHAT OTHER WILL NOT,
SO YOU CAN LIVE TOMORROW AS OTHERS CANNOT

DREAMS ARE WHAT FUTURES ARE MADE OF

IF YOU FAIL TO PLAN YOU PLAN TO FAIL

DREAMS DON'T ALWAYS END WHEN YOU WAKE UP

LOOK AT ALL THE GREAT INVENTIONS IN THE WORLD.
THEY ALL STARTED WITH A DREAM

DREAMS ARE WHEN YOU IMAGINE BIG.
REALITIES ARE BIG IMAGINATIONS COME TRUE

Description of My Dream

Place photograph
or
picture here

use paper or craft glue

Date Set

Date Achieved

Goals & Plans
What I will do to achieve my dream.

Notes

**HANG AROUND DREAMERS AND YOUR DREAMS WILL BECOME A REALITY – GUARANTEED!
HANG AROUND DREAM STEALERS AND YOUR DREAMS WILL REMAIN DREAMS – UNACHIEVED!!**

Description of My Dream

Place photograph
or
picture here

use paper or craft glue

Date Set

Date Achieved

Goals & Plans
What I will do to achieve my dream.

Notes

WHEN YOUR DREAMS SEEM SO FAR AWAY, RESET THE GOALS AND KEEP GOING

Description of My Dream

Place photograph
or
picture here

use paper or craft glue

Date Set

Date Achieved

Goals & Plans
What I will do to achieve my dream.

Notes

Description of My Dream

Place photograph
or
picture here

use paper or craft glue

Date Set

Date Achieved

Goals & Plans
What I will do to achieve my dream.

Notes

Description of My Dream

Place photograph
or
picture here

use paper or craft glue

Date Set

Date Achieved

Goals & Plans
What I will do to achieve my dream.

Notes

DREAMS ARE WHAT YOU BUILD YOUR FUTURE ON
SO MAKE SURE YOUR FUTURE IS FILLED WITH DREAMS COME TRUE

Description of My Dream

Place photograph
or
picture here

use paper or craft glue

Date Set

Date Achieved

Goals & Plans
What I will do to achieve my dream.

Notes

Description of My Dream

Date Set

Date Achieved

place photograph
or
picture here

Goals & Plans
What I will do to achieve my dream

Description

Notes

MAKE YOUR DREAM PLAIN TO SEE, SO YOU KNOW WHAT TO KEEP YOUR EYES ON

Description of My Dream

Place photograph
or
picture here

use paper or craft glue

Date Set

Date Achieved

Goals & Plans
What I will do to achieve my dream.

Notes

OBSTACLES WILL BE IN YOUR WAY
GO AROUND THEM, THROUGH THEM, BUT JUST KEEP GOING

Description of My Dream

Place photograph
or
picture here

use paper or craft glue

Date Set

Date Achieved

Goals & Plans
What I will do to achieve my dream.

Notes

DON'T LET ANY THING STOP YOU FROM DOING WHAT YOU NEED TO DO

Description of My Dream

Place photograph
or
picture here

use paper or craft glue

Date Set

Date Achieved

Goals & Plans
What I will do to achieve my dream.

Notes

Description of My Dream

Place photograph
or
picture here

use paper or craft glue

Date Set

Date Achieved

Goals & Plans
What I will do to achieve my dream.

Notes

Description of My Dream

Place photograph
or
picture here

use paper or craft glue

Date Set

Date Achieved

Goals & Plans
What I will do to achieve my dream.

Notes

Description of My Dream

Place photograph
or
picture here

use paper or craft glue

Date Set

Date Achieved

Goals & Plans
What I will do to achieve my dream.

Notes

THINK BEYOND, GO BEYOND AND LIVE BEYOND ANY DREAM YOU HAVE

Description of My Dream

Place photograph
or
picture here

use paper or craft glue

Date Set

Date Achieved

Goals & Plans
What I will do to achieve my dream.

Notes

DON'T LAUGH AT SOMEONE ELSE'S DREAM BUT ENCOURAGE AND UPLIFT THEM, JUST AS YOU WOULD WANT THEM TO DO TO YOU

Description of My Dream

Place photograph
or
picture here

use paper or craft glue

Date Set

Date Achieved

Goals & Plans
What I will do to achieve my dream.

Notes

DON'T JUST WISH YOUR DREAM, MAKE YOUR DREAM HAPPEN!

Description of My Dream

Place photograph
or
picture here

use paper or craft glue

Date Set

Date Achieved

Goals & Plans
What I will do to achieve my dream.

Notes

**A PASSION FOR A DREAM CAN LIFT YOUR SPIRIT
BUT WITH NO PASSION AND NO DREAM, YOUR SPIRIT IS DESTROYED**

Description of My Dream

Place photograph
or
picture here

use paper or craft glue

Date Set

Date Achieved

Goals & Plans
What I will do to achieve my dream.

Notes

THE ONLY PERSON WHO CAN STOP YOU IS YOU

Description of My Dream

Place photograph
or
picture here

use paper or craft glue

Date Set

Date Achieved

Goals & Plans
What I will do to achieve my dream.

Notes

DREAMS DON'T ALWAYS END WHEN YOU WAKE UP

Description of My Dream

Place photograph
or
picture here

use paper or craft glue

Date Set

Date Achieved

Goals & Plans
What I will do to achieve my dream.

Notes

LOOK AT ALL THE GREAT INVENTIONS IN THE WORLD.
THEY ALL STARTED WITH A DREAM

Description of My Dream

Place photograph
or
picture here

use paper or craft glue

Date Set

Date Achieved

Goals & Plans
What I will do to achieve my dream.

Notes